9/00

IN ANOTHER COUNTRY

by

Gerry Wells

Typeset and Published
by
The National Poetry Foundation
(Reg Charity No 283032)
27 Mill Road
Fareham
Hants PO16 0TH
(Tel: 0329 822218)

Printed by
Meon Valley Printers
Bishops Waltham (0489 895460)

Sponsored by Rosemary Arthur

Cover Photograph by Celia Rambaut

For Gill – with love

'Boys In The Blackberry Woods' was a prize–winner in the Peterloo Poetry Competition, 1990.

Poems in this book have also appeared in: *Envoi, Arvon Anthology 1987, Proof, Sol, Poetry Matters, Ore, Arts Council Anthology 8, Wordshare, Working Titles, Iota, The Frogmore Papers, Bradford Poetry Quarterly, New Poetry, Outposts, Poetry & Audience* and *Foolscap*.

ISBN 1 870556 46 1

£4.00

CONTENTS

* * *

ACOUSTICS

Epidaurus, its concavity
to hold thousands; the first
stone lifted and space hewn
smoking out of Hades. Each
breath's labouring arrival
breathed history older, its earth
bladed to the bone – till tamed,
tiered, a stage was set.

You leave, go elegantly down
each tier of fifty–nine,
skirt swinging as you count,
I count, each one – till
you arrive, assume all stage
in the scented stillness.

                    A cicada
rasps distantly – then you speak,
Clytemnestra speaks...
Agamemnon is back from Troy.

You, solitary,
your pain–instrument of words
flights upwards, image after image –
each bell–syllable shock clear,
chill as deepest water.

GONE WEST

Time separates: the twelve–hour flight
breaks up congruence;
now I occupy a day
that you exchanged for night.

Here hill–crests shape the sky
and meditate; early there was rain –
but now the scent of steaming road
and wet dust turning dry

and oddly, oranges – first seen
as painted suns against their green.

All this existing as you rest
curled warmly under winter
and the likelihood of frost.

We are weather–man and wife, alone,
one out, one done,
predicting snow, predicting sun –

for such is this experience, day's light
on my shoulder, you darkly asleep.
distances are definite.

SUN, SHADOW AND LEAF

The sun-repeated cypresses
give teeth to the track, shade
a courtyard, its cracked stone table
and broken seats;

                    how still
the afternoon. I try to write you
something memorable, my stanzas
patrolled by ants;

but thought is slow, so many years
raked-up like leaves, elude –
wait for a fire, the first cold wind.

I lean on elbows, rock
a sleepy rhythm and all is ordered –
sun and shade, a track
that wars have passed along,
and silence.

            Then,
beyond my feet, close –
a Tuscan viper,
his chain-mail summer dusty,
engrossed in warmth.

He's danger, real –
but peaceful on his land
and I intrude,
worse, failed to see him

and what else among those tidied leaves?

3

GOING HOME

When the dawn ran red as a fox,
you woke – saying we must go home
so you could die; we had delayed
through perfect Tuscan days for that.

Later, jolting down mule–brained tracks
homewards, past two beached villages,
you made me stop.

The cut engine left such stillness –
a silence luminous with broom;
behind us a farmhouse crumbled,
blind of eye, a slack door hanging

waiting for winds –
a slow regression, explaining
dumbly the soil had been too thin.

Standing   apart,
in pain–created privacy,
you held your sickness like a child,
oblivious of the farm, and looked

away beyond the ochre field
littered with dead vine, travelling
further than anyone might see.

With your death past premonition,
it seemed that those moments pulled you
root by root, not in regression,
but like the late swift in summer,

restless in blue inviting air,
shaping to fly to other gods
more perfectly perceived than mine.

I lost you then.

ON THE FIRST DAY

After the rope has broken – shock.
(What does the climber think about
before he hits rock?)

Now you have gone, that look –
the rare theme of you
closed like a book;

so they attend you quietly there,
straightening your curled body,
tidying your hair.

What matters now is nothing matters,
apprehension deceives like water
suggesting depths, a glitter

of perception peculiar to the eye –
sun going behind a pleat of cloud,
a milk–float going by,

each thing detatched, part of a scene
that comes up out of distance
as if you had never been.

The climber only spins
past sharpened images, then it is over.
What is to come, begins.

DIGGING THE EARLIES

The worked earth is warm, new
like resurrection from a country
as far away as winter. You
mothered it, set the roots exactly,
mindful of their green emerging
and that pleasure – flowering.

Life has driven deep since then –
and in that blind interim awoke
from mud its stars. Your blade bright
on clods that once were skylines broke
down the timeless – but earth won't wait,
regroups its armies grain by grain.

A slow becoming to this time –
with your fork deep-buried, one
eager hand tight round a haulm
in unison of thrust and pull
and upturn to a clustered spill...
this brim of nuggets in the sun.

Stooping you indulge, aware
of each smoothness, its pungency,
your fingers recording there
these children out of potent darks.
You brush your newborn lightly free –
knowing how all this process works.

WAITING FOR THE NIGHT TRAIN

You might guess he never made it
from the start, never the child
puking and pram-safe, assuming
sustinence, even love – already
shrunk from the calamitous egg
to his own grey ghost.

                How long
before premonition ripened
in the muddy dregs of bad wine,
the first mainline jabbed retreat –
reclaiming him, scar by scar?

Cankered,   simian,
he drags his shadow to where we sit,
stands in vigil on the cigarette
clipped smoking in your hand.
                   Ravenous.

Embarrassed, you drop it in the tray –
it's gone – to lip, to whole body...

He drifts back,
garbage to the beach, glaring
his vernacular – "fuck you asshole..."
blasting from the depths of him,
a mantra.

Turning away,
the whole epic of himself,
his stink's an accusation
trailed behind.

THE ONES BETWEEN

Bloodshot moments, brute
densities, swatched colours
dripping still...TORIES OUT!

Police reinforcements fill
the square, baton clashing shield.
a Xingu rhythm, tribal...

and this boy of the stamping foot
noting our Happy Chinese Eater
doorway – with us locked out...

                        scaffolding,
a lance of it, strikes tarmac,
jangles, ricocheting hate
at him like flak...

the two of him, boy marching,
boy running scared,
his baton in between;

a zoom–shot scene:
fate's finger on the button
plays through the dream

we action in slow motion here –
bottles held in flight, sun–
shards poised in jellied air,

his baton arcing, weightless
till it strikes – his own fear
his enforcement: the very best.

ON THE CIRCLE LINE

The day's first train is waiting:
we settle in the bitter tang
of vomit and pumped air.
Cross–legged, one man tin–
whistles night–time out of ear:
he's slept rough, if slept at all,
this piping oracle.

Reckon him in centuries – that
face played dreams at Agincourt
(bowstring safely under cap, his
lice asleep); the tunes float
pulsing through the business
of being here. Travelling man,
he comes once, comes never again.

He toys with lament then brings out
childhood, fragile notes that beat
across the space of memory;
the doors finally slide shut –
platform, people, go slipping by
the window like a film. Frame
by frame he pipes us away.

HURRY ON HOME

Hard to believe
at this shrivelled end of autumn,
there's a clutch of pippins on a bare-
branched tree, painted sunsets alive
in a sting of rain;

                while somewhere
sharp-sounding like Notting Hill
or Acton where hard men still
prop their houses up and stare,
Pizarro in a flash of Rolls veers
from rush-hour traffic, to turn
a not-so-streetwise pigeon
into rosy floating feathers
the wipers take time to clear:
a four-fifteen horizon
lies straight ahead, stretched-out
and golden...keeps his foot clamped down,
the pleasures short.

              Further on,
a well-oiled river slips to the sea,
steals gold impressions of the sky,
a clutch of sunsets, on its run –
ferries them away.

BEACH GAMES

Emphatic place, a mood of emptiness,
of space – nothing either way,
the sea sluiced-off an east horizon.

Reaction is to walk as converstion
flags; they've done religion and
what they've learned (quite personal),

now he'd like to say, "You're beautiful" –
but the wind's too full of icy rivets
for artless observations.

So they examine shells, the curly ones
you hear the sea in, make it to Mablethorpe
across a stage of sand.

Reason takes it in the end,
the logic of the outer senses damps
the silly warmth of passion;

how the state of truth surprises! In procession
the seabirds fly back from land, groups
of waders stab at their reflections

while a running tide of demons
swirls its gritty water ankle-deep,
making people islands.

FLORENTINES

A square whitened by the moon:
La Piazza della Signoria; in
the shadows Savanarola still
screams, but he's centuries gone –
reduced by fire, a spectacle.

A melt–down history, something
to pick at and match a nagging fear:
I at this high window, you brooding –
calmly mirror–imaged and combing,
a thousand miles from here.

We assassinate ourselves, a game
bodied by imagination – obsessed
as moths going for a flame
to check it's real, depressed
when it burns. Impasse.

Chains fix me to a stake:
I cannot touch or speak –
tonight we're doomed to thrash
the edge of bed. A frisson leaks
in from the dark, brings a hint of ash.

I go to clean my teeth and play
the night's defence – then..."Shit!
I've lost my toothbrush..." words ahead of thought –
cathartic as a shattering plate.

"Use mine," you say.

SETTLING THE FIRSTBORN - FOR GILL

Proclaiming in profanity...
her voice plaits stillness
twist by twist, with agonies
she finds in what she is,

her angry fingers testing
your shirt like braille,
as if to seize a meaning
from the weft of wool.

Somnambulistic, patiently,
you hear the ticking dialect
of dark hours, till close by
the first bird unbuds light –

infinite, a distillation
caught in measures to fill
heart and ear – a late migration
homing–in like love, one frail

voice beginning where we begin,
the many motes of us who float
to brief significance then drift on –
travellers and those who wait...

She quietens now, takes fragile
hold on sleep, assigning future,
its possibility, to you: arrival –
the two of you, together.

DÉJÀ VU

Weak sun through glass, vague
lit patterns of other men
stain his hands as if to warm;
outside, a bland skyline –
tumps and tumours of a time
lapsed by plague.

He broods; the church is cold again,
empty of parent, guest. Gripped
now by this need to think, to make clear
his taking of the child, cradling
her – and as always, fear
he might let her slip.
                    She had wailed,
thin sounds clinging to air
like birds; water beaded her skin
then, named, she lay bright as a flower
holding his eye. Such strangeness! Fire
burned through the moment, held, then
dwindled to dark, a shot star...
and he knowing – *this we have done
as if destined,*
                    but somehow failed –
to repeat again and again.

He sees altar, pulpit, adze–marked weight
of forest – symbols on a page
of text, that oaken pull
at certainty; but this frail image
from a far dream takes all his heart –
traveller without certainty, a blip
on a screen homing still.
Time plays back: the cradled face looks up.

15

BOYS IN THE BLACKBERRY WOODS

The sun hangs his hawk on a string –
slips through slates of leaf, burns
water-green a kingdom. The trees sing;

hand-to-mouth, they're struck...might
be comic statues cocked to this tune
inviting deeper rides of appetite:

pied as the piper, an insurgent
flighting the blood and brain.
They loiter edgily, silent

as victims unearthed by some forest god
who jokingly sprouts each one
his horns, his cleft foot – manhood

in too small a vessel. But a joke's
a joke...this god quiets the siren
trees, generously gives back

the schoolroom world – though they won't forget,
but puzzle as at a dream, then
flesh it out. One day to enter it.

HOT AIR BALLOONS

Vagrant as blown seed, they bring
a potency to early morning
and our village; on my shoulders
a weighty daughter savours
the word..."balloo...oons" – then, "What
(inevitable question) makes them float?"
I grapple with the physics
of ascent, those grotesque cheeks
blown tight by an orange jet
blasting air a million candles hot.

"But Daddy, they're coming down!"
Indeed they are, one in Jack Straw's corn,
the others with tact and much more grace
unzip their waistcoats into space
he reaped and ploughed a week ago,
their laundry baskets spilling crew
and laughter; my daughter bounces: "They'll all
want their breakfast now!" Perhaps they will
but, all things considered, I doubt
if Jack Straw's good for anything like that.

Balloons, they take her with them all day long,
gaudy–striped and chequered, down
the winding valleys of her mind, till they
arrive at bed–time – their paunched memory
drifting overhead: "Daddy, those seeds –
will they grow flowers?" She doesn't need
an answer...from her pinch of candle–flame
she fires the colours of a dream,
floats into sleep.

A TIME OF YEAR

Focus – a still absorption...
her transistor's playing
something   Lennon;

Park–space hallucinates
fairground yellow, reds,
spring and roundabouts.

She, baby at breast
nipple–tight, in prairie
daisies – the two of them
and Lennon.

          Old men sit along
the tennis courts: sap rises,
their sticks sprout daffodils;
they wipe their eyes.

Out there in early sun –
timeless mother, child,
in pose that warms cathedrals.

Pietà update.

THE DRIFTER

Now this man escaping, lolls
warm on glittery waves; a wind
takes him gently; gently pulls
him from far crowds on the sand –
where wife tans and his shrill
children dig among thousands.

He takes on a dream, riding
his raft's lolloping stripes,
a mending dream to make living
better than new. A gull dips
clean on a fine wing, fleeting
a shadow at the edge of sleep;

he sloughs–off the world in its skin,
flat–backed on an easy sea.
In fathoms where imagination
broods, a breath of current softly
rises off its shoal, conniving, then
drifts dream and man away.

A crest of air chills through to bone;
he wakes, ferried on a flat
mile–deep dark that bled the sun –
sees land lights sprinkle on a far track,
orbiting as tides take hold. Now this man
escaping, thinks to travel back...

CLEARING UP

The shelves crowd us in, leather Tort
and Common Law shack-up together;
a fly does his feet on the window.
"Blah," says your solicitor, earning
his hundred guineas.

We understand him perfectly,
two accomplished enemies
across a table – once rooted oak,
a sky behind its leaves.

We sign the settled peace. I sign,
you sign, the oak straining in the wind.
It's dusty quiet, the fly departs.

But I see, with shock, your finger
without our ring – and an epoch's sealed.

A future, till now unthought,
draws up beside me.

ON THE WAY FROM THE PAINT SHOP

Tyrannosaurus Rex – on show,
(our greatest electronic feat),
grins razor from his flat-
bed truck: secured, he checks-out
a latitude that dumped him long ago.

Along the teeming highway a fume
of burned-up ancient forest stings
the air – but that unblinking eye
red-reflecting our lowered beam,
calculates with brute reasoning
how long fear might fix this prey.

Grown gargantuan he sways
uneasily, goes ranging straight
into that bitter long-lapsed war
that brought him down: what furies
beset that tiny brain when armour
proved no safe-conduct, when climate,
whole continents, slid away...
                                    treacheries
to engorge his whole gross weight.

We keep station on his truck
this warm December evening; the sick
earth under San Francisco quakes
while we go on trailing him back.

Getting on to the interstate
Friday p.m. – late. Anger takes
toll of another week gone sour:
the typist, out of love, working
too slowly at your mistakes,
your whole career
hanging by a string.

Two such, too close, turn
as bulls to a riverbank,
miscalculate (again) and run
together already ragged flanks.

That's it.

They swerve,
pull in where they shouldn't stop.
Their week hits its peak raw nerve.

"You blind or something, asshole?"
"Don't asshole me, you asshole –"
dialogue of ritual
focused on itself, the stake...
The grinning traffic
drenches by what is cathartic
but sadly absurd, a play
geared tautly up to make
another weekend seem okay,

Until,

a too–close state patrol
noses from a side–street –
but by now they're off the hook,
the week safe down its hole;
but they still move fast, the book
would be one more defeat.

They head downtown, their ways
cut in a fast–lane Porsche;
its managing director removing
hand from typist's knee, braking –
passes managerial thought:
"Assholes," he says.

AT THE WHARF

A big tourist's sun slicks
oiled water; a fisherman
kneeling to bait-up his hooks
curses the sea-lions that come
grunting from the same drowned world
we brought our own blood from.

All day they'd drift and pick
at gifts of squid (just 50 cents a bag),
but for the gulls' dipped-in-ochre beaks:
flying low, they keep the sun behind,
each buttoned eye tight-stitched
to a rent collector's mind –
raucous above the swell,
its moat of supplicants
silly as people.

50 cents of processed gut
and squid flips up and out... a gull,
ten gulls drop, stabbing at air –
a buoyed head ducks. Meanwhile,
a jolly tripper crowding back,
tosses-up another lot...
a gull, ten gulls drop
in contemptuous spirals,
perfecting the act.

AIRFIELD

As seen on t.v.: war left to rot
beneath a sagging height
of hangar close by cut–
off runways. It's late.

Cliché stuff: soon we'll hear
Lancasters (most with an engine shot) –
and see through smoky darkness a flare
go up...fall and go out;

a frequent happening,
taking the time of happening –

but it's minds now, not sky, those bombers cross –
and the moment's passed;
we ride on, some farmer's sugarbeet
vivid   underfoot.

In this dimming fall
of evening, thinking's not original,
merely reminds us that when we're gone
we're gone –
that only echoes hold
on to outlines across the field,

while those planes hang on the wind –
stacked–up   survivors
still flying out of legend
under the cold blink of stars.

BARBARIANS

Caesar's edict is austere –
"Prepare, the barbarian is near..."

Stakes are driven, the earthworks done,
ordnance and war–machine secure,
the troops morose at maintenance;
a missile honed to brightness
takes an edge of sun.

Groups of women outside sing
in a shrill release of sound,
as fatigue groups tear down their tents –
a weekly happening.

Silent legionaries stare
(their faces tell one nothing),
but the Centurion frets, men
gone off the boil are worrying,
there should be no women there.

In the watch past sunset,
a reflected scarlet from the women's fires
stains cloud, a gale blasts off
some glacier grinding south; yet

a rampart guard takes stock – eye
and imagination's stagecraft shape
the barbarian he expects, play
at more than Caesar's shadowing
in a theatre of sky.

Up into cloud and the wind bites,
the jeep bucking on frozen mud; twenty
miles away as the shell flies,
you could cool your feet in the sea.

Phoenicians used caves up here (to avoid
the Greeks) – while they built an alphabet,
words seeming more useful than the sword;
we pass a temple, one column still erect.

Cloud filters the sun; we hesitate near
soldiers, one waves us by, his image fixed
as on a photographic plate in sepia,
stilled to recollection as we relax.

After descent, noon saturates the eye,
jungle swarms around the cedar, its
shadows go about uneasily.
A car–bomb takes out a block of flats.

Under the sun and the factions' feet
the absent seed lays down its root
in darkness, destined for light
and flowering again; but not yet.

FIELDCRAFT FOR BEGINNERS

Without it you won't survive.

The course is all uphill,
its problems, original.

To summarise:

use dead ground if you can,
as does the fox
who makes for safety on a run –
think of it as paradox;
never break a skyline
or you're done.

Make the most of stillness
but be circumspect,
as with the skater's ice
it's hard to predict.

When you feel,
do it deeply – be
the camouflaging tree,
use all its colour, note
how live things yield,
adapt to dark and light,
the elusive line
that moves – and stills again;

be subtle, come
gently to the time of taking,
like autumn,
and flexible – never go
against it, ride the blow,
that quick turn in stride
will keep you moving
and alive.

Now all the stage is yours,
the training's ended;
when you hit those boards
hit them fast, down and away
as if your life depended:

it does. Today.

PUMP AND PRECINCT

Curlicued, the manor's
gift to a grateful hamlet:
state–of–the–art cast iron,
squealed blurts of sun
up from an ice–age, fire-
spun cold; sweet.

Wallflowers gifting stone
and still air, the slabs worn
shiny by armies – Waterloo to
Somme via bloody Prussians:
old men forget, or never knew,
whole generations...

on watch for cottage women,
the young ones coming down
for water – a run gauntlet,
but they knew, flounced
wit and oaken bucket
while sun–chips danced;

gargoyled, the troops
mopped and dickered,
died in heaps.

The well's dry now, no war
worth mentioning for years,
nor wallflower either –

pump's a wigged Georgian
crowned with a can.

30

FISHERMAN'S PUB

Fish hooks, flies – high–coloured ticklers –
walls the colour of Cadbury's Plain:
Red Lion and the Saturday regulars
watch another week out. Dai, bone–thin,

too old for sheep, twitches under my chair
far mountains away. Rheumatic Jem talks
fishing, bloody trippers, the local fair
next weekend. A lad from the village chalks

up double twenty. Double images
these: all the changes leaving things the same
are here. The talk in different languages
weaving, fills out an unremitting game.

Jem clears the ashtrays – and from the bridge
tips fag–end débris down to the Teifi,
then leans a moment on the evening's edge,
silent; a crisp–bag lodges in the ivy.

Double top is finished, ashtrays shine,
the changing and the changeless blend to ring
the players on this stage; fresh off some skyline
Tom, shepherd, takes his teeth out, starts to sing.

THE CASTLE FACTOR

Uneasy in translation, the scrawl:
Visitors are asked to avoid accidents
sets the mind to a cascade of summer
dress and camera over the walls.

What reputation the place has grown,
gesturing behind gross towers
at yet another upstart century
come to goggle at its bones.

What remains is under tight control,
but there's brokenness blocked-in
behind the thin Welsh sunlight –
Llewellyn still sizes-up a village girl
for the stinking bracken of his couch,
and there hangs that thunderous
spiral blackness on the staircase
we're not allowed to reach.

History never dies. Articulate,
it mortared love and hate enough
into the stone's bleak language,
grows fat on legend as it waits.

Our guide moves on, we pause –
then silence shuts hard down behind...
out of loitering dark, armies detach
and move towards us, unsheathing swords.

FROM A PAINTING BY WYETH

Regeneration seems not to be the theme –
pine trees in hippo hides move
in open order along a track

and someone with a sense of place
has set an upturned helmet
in the shadow of a branch,

filled it with dry cones;

feeble sunlight, dead needles
fallen to an early frost
complete a frame of stillness

which could be anywhere that
history speaks of, or merely
where such trees grow.

That re–filled military relic
denotes its cause, complete
with empty riches,

the seed long gone.

CLIMBING MOUNTAINS

Two hours upward on the trail
with mist a slack tide over
the stone history of Wales.

Climbing, our voices go out
echoing over mountain
drops and darkness. Underfoot

the great carcass moves, an old
hide shivering as it takes
us through the wet kiss of cloud,

its vernacular a raw
chaotic beauty driving
us on and higher past sheer

fantasies of space filling
pink with dawn, until we reach
that place where time goes spilling

into nothingness. Legend
still speaks of one man who stood
high on this rock in storm winds,

straight as a pole, to answer
for his dreams – till he was struck
by a single bolt of fire.

Such the tale. That gift we search
for perhaps was his – a bright
implosion with earth, sky, each

newly made before he fell;
few can steal fire from heaven
and survive – while others still

stand chained to failure shaped by
need – sharp now, vital as these
quick shadows the ravens fly.

THE WAITING GAME

The ferry's gone. We wait.
In the glittery light
a glimpsed something moves,
mobbed by waves.

Wind stropping the leather
of our faces, we can do no more
than stare and speculate; a cry,
a chip of sound, jars distantly.

Then rising in silhouette
a wing shapes up in quirky bat–
flight, jinking to skid on air,
jockeying some horror

a feather's lift away:
not drowning, that osprey
makes trial of strength, wars
with an attrition no prayers

can alter...the solitary
who drops to tread his silky
mistress who can't escape –
servant till his first mistake.

CLIMBING IN GREECE

Toe–deep on the face he
traverses, his feet step
lightly; fingers crawl a grip
on spur and concavity.

Stillness shatters, a grate
of débris, struck notes
falling: behind – ten feet of ledge is space...

Tenuously his route leads on
towards an image of tomorrow,
its possibility – the only one.
Finally he moves to force fixed
muscles to the immediacy of *now* –
this first step...then the next;

a cicada falls, clings to a fragment
inches from his eye: it's dusted black
from summer fires, but the music's
vibrant – "tzitzik...tzitzik...tzitzik..."
fixing each moment.

FOREST FIRE

Sun through glass, its eye
focused: heat spawning...
the gene flowers, hungry.

Fire, you're free! Break
through sleeping acres
before enemies strike back,

outflanking you. Your brothers,
idle behind bars, will know
your far voice, its rumours –

and sing. Now all wilderness,
thicket and pine, are yours...
call–up the wind, mistress

to give you children
out of murderous air
with love, easy and often:

hunt through feasts
of kingdoms,
breathe forests.

BUILDING IN STONE

Higher than the buttresses,
the way to glory under heel,
Matthew builds in stone –
lays down history from a greater one;
his angles, perpendiculars,
are true, block on block –
huge and pulling at the eye.

Fate and legend lie strong
in that cropped head;
if he feels pain
he keeps it to himself;
if he praises
it is through the stroke of steel
into unwilling stone.

Through the winter of a year
the symbol grows,
Ark–like on another Ararat;
with the spire comes marvelling
and talk of miracles.

Over the hovels sharp chippings fly
as men like Matthew
fashion the character of faith –
thought clotted to the pitch
and poise of balance,

eye to eye with an ice–hearted wind,
in the company of angels.

CANDLES

Candles come out like stars,
print echoes on the cloudy air
and draw the grateful eye, the hand
to surprising warmth; people group around.

It's like this always when shadows move
toward you over stone, the nave
they come from conceals a filling tide,
a nothingness that comes alive.

Time at sunset aggregates unrest –
at this opaqueness on the move, the fust
that history smells of in cathedral air;
dark's the abstract of our fear.

It's the medieval in us, the Faustus flaw
that lights our candle, locks the door.

EASTER PROCESSION

For as long as they've had to wait
they've waited – the women veiled,
young girls in white.

A priest intones, stirring
air as a breeze through corn,
cloud–shadows racing...

The great arena fills:
alchemy of sunlight – carmine,
shifting tints of amber, purples...

blessing each one who goes aisle–bent
into atmospheric distances –
serenely moving, obedient

to the call, its vernacular
invoking no vain images –
acoustic   metaphor.

For us, a sense of loss. Colours fade;
sly cameras whisper to seize what's left
from the rainbow's other side.

SOMETHING FROM THE SCROLLS

A stranger came down from the hills
great falcon on wrist, hooded
as his eyes were hooded, stood
on the periphery of our lives,
and watched.

In the heat of noon
he released the falcon,
it rose cloud high, a mobile
hung from the sun,
and stooped –
struck at the blind eye of a man
in the shadows
asleep.

We look up from the blood
dark in the dust,
see the blue hills
and footprints to them;
if he comes in the dawn
from those hills again,

we shall offer him water.

NOTES ON THE HUNTER

Tigers circle in his head,
a rolling gait of day on day,
while thirsty herds of clichés
trail down goat-paths to the pub.

Mock-gothic poxed with stucco,
this old thicket of jungle
holds the hunter and his prey –
both clotted into silence
round another empty glass.

When this waterhole dries up
he'll die, though not from thirst,
but quickly and with panache
in stripping mirage from chaste lands –
finding that last image, exploding,
to be real and pure and endless...

ON THE EDGE

The Saxon abacus and arch
made their impact – but he
needed Naseby...

So we took the longer way
and stood where Cromwell
bloodied that summer day.

It's heartland, he studied it –
that long slope ideal for cavalry,
then hedgerow and the wide fields' symmetry;

how different then, a moor scoured by the wind,
boggy. He assessed it all again –
attack, pursuit, by men well disciplined:

"Cromwell led them from the front – that's good,
sharing men's danger earns respect,
we need our battlefields and blood."

He was silent then, the country slept...
while the troopers of his army
sat their horses restlessly,

counting intolerable odds.

AN INNOCENT AT THE PARTY

Everyone's   invited,
nobody   permitted
the   least   excuse...
I   refill   my   glass.

Our   host   is   late   they   say,
meanwhile   this   house
is   ours   entirely,   for   us
to   make   the   most   of   and   enjoy.

We   do: each   face   –   known,
unknown,   deep   in   champagne,
real   ale,   even   exotic   teas...
hallucinating   pleasantly.

Party   mood   ignites: where
one   hears   silence,   voices   slip
in   round   it,   as   to   a   mishap,
printing   the   air;

through   the   window   a   new   moon
turns   our   small   change   over,
not   quite   jokingly;   one   by   one
familiars   disappear.

My   last   good   companion
gives   me   his   glass,
"Hang   on   to   this,   old   man   –
shan't   be   a   sec..."   reels   breathless
to   a   door   opening   into   dark;
I   hang   on,   await   his   coming   back.

IN ANOTHER COUNTRY

Far away, a light –
briefly. A house? Is not,
is star briefly caught
then quenched by night
or skyline. His stalled

car seems derelict in a cold
that breathes across the field
into his ear; spinneys of felled
larch loom resinous nearby, spilled
shadows bleeding white as moon

through cloud. Without a phone
this man recalls the nearest one
ten miles away, a limp snake slung
behind smashed glass – but seen
then merely as some crass joke.

He takes lengthy stock,
beached in darkness – a dark
of emanation having little truck
with town suburb or its slick
estate: a kingdom of the blind –

that darkest quarter when hand
leads eye with history on the wind,
its presence underfoot and all around –
a seeming enemy destined to stand
ready on hostile borders. Fed

by indecision, he's afraid to tread
this foreign stillness fom outside
reason, its muttering of war. Afraid –
but fear creates the enemy men need:
he leaves the car, steps out ahead.

CITY

Then, as now, the heat...

traders in the square
voice a coinage of echoes
along the colonnades, ears gathering,
the hand stretched out.

Zeus, nucleus of faith, pulls the sky
to temple tile and pediment,
the city is matter radiating
into mirage.

Way and highway empty at noon
into bawdy-house and stable
and the musky shade; indolence
sleeps between lovers.

There was a crucifixion after dawn,
the clump of mallet
driving spikes
and other sounds.

Meridian is now:

the spread shadow
draws to the root of agony,
the air too fierce for anything
but silence.

A skyline covers the sun,
rituals of necessity resume
as shod wheels grieve
late home from Tiberias.

Now, as then, the heat...

barbarian time broke down the gates,
Zeus and Artemis are sunk
statuary among stones –
things ceasing to be things,

as burned–up grasses
rub the air like crickets.

What moment left this city dead?

EXPATRIATES

White-crusted villas, a line
iced thickly on the cake of Spain...
another day; a servant flogs
at a pair of Moroccan rugs –
but even sound moves slowly here:
her stick falls, then what seems a year
goes by before the thump-thump flops
down dead among the patio pots.

Our neighbours are still asleep,
their baked bodies under a sheet
and the scent of coffee. Later
they'll emerge, start-up the Rover
and drive off down the hill to town
and supermarket. Met him on his own
last week, in the Little England part
where rows of Haig and Gordon's wait.

"It's OK here, old boy. Just keep
your money off-shore and speak
the lingo – well anyway, enough
for what you need. Oh yes, the wife
loves gardening, it keeps her fit.
I do a bit of pruning to help out,
pay-off the bills occasionally –
they're no problem here. It'll do me,
and bugger Britain, the country's done."

We quaked our spotted hands towards the gin.